Original title:
Shadows in the Shrubbery

Copyright © 2025 Creative Arts Management OÜ
All rights reserved.

Author: Jameson Hartfield
ISBN HARDBACK: 978-1-80567-344-6
ISBN PAPERBACK: 978-1-80567-643-0

Murmurs Across the Garden's Edge

In the corner, whispers giggle,
Little creatures dance and wiggle.
A hedgehog hums a silly tune,
While flowers laugh beneath the moon.

Bamboo sways with gentle grace,
As bugs take part in a wacky race.
With every rustle, secrets spill,
Each tiny noise a joyful thrill.

Laced with Secrets of the Wild

The squirrels plot with beady eyes,
While crafty crows rehearse their lies.
A gopher digs, his tales untruth,
And sings of gardens filled with ruth.

But vines unravel, laughter spread,
As undergrowth turns bright and red.
With nature's jest, the game's afoot,
In tangled leaves, they all stay put.

Dappled Light and Dark Visions

Amidst the blooms, a rabbit pranced,
He tripped on roots and quite a glance.
With floppy ears and silly hops,
He turned his fall to belly flops.

A mischievous breeze, the butterflies laugh,
In this wacky world, there's no tough path.
Leaves fall down like tiny stuck clowns,
Who knew the garden wore funny gowns?

Breach of Light in the Overgrowth

Through tangle green, daylight spills,
Caterpillars spin their funny frills.
With each bright hue, there's laughter near,
Even the weeds seem giddy here.

A snail in shades, slow but sly,
Watches as butterflies dance and fly.
In the thicket, joy is found,
Where every turn brings a silly sound.

Silhouettes Amidst the Thickets

Little figures dash and play,
Hiding where the twigs do sway.
Giggles echo, spirits spry,
Wobbling like a dancing pie.

Squirrels don a clever mask,
In the leaves, they slyly bask.
Whispers float on breezy trails,
Crafty creatures tell tall tales.

The bushes whisper secrets bright,
As furry pals take to flight.
Bouncing off the leafy beds,
With acorn hats upon their heads.

Twisting shapes with comical flair,
Lurking with the utmost care.
In this green, a raucous jest,
Who knew plants could be so blessed?

Echoes of Twilight in the Green

Beneath the trees where giggles spring,
Mischief plays on sprightly wing.
A tap-dancing owl strikes a pose,
With knobbly knees and a nose that glows.

Crickets gather, a band so keen,
Creating music seldom seen.
Their chirps unite in jovial cheer,
As moonlit beams draw the night near.

A raccoon in a top hat prances,
Leading his friends in silly dances.
With each twirl, a rustle is made,
While beetles join, unafraid.

Just beyond where the nightbirds sing,
Laughter rises, a playful thing.
Here, the dusk becomes a game,
Twisted antics, never the same!

Ghostly Forms Among the Boughs

Mischief stirs amid the leaves,
Where ghoulish giggles weave and cleave.
Glowing eyes peer from the night,
In a dance of frightful delight.

The bushes jolt with every sound,
As playful phantoms loop around.
In this odd enchanted maze,
They frolic in a silly haze.

A hedgehog dons a ghostly shroud,
Daring to be bold, not cowed.
With puffs of air, the leaves collide,
As frothy laughter fills the tide.

Swirling forms in midnight fun,
They spin and bounce till night is done.
Among the boughs, a jolly scene,
Who knew the night could be so keen?

The Dance of Dusk on the Leaves

With each step, the branches sway,
As critters gather for a play.
Fireflies blink in wild romance,
Inviting all to join the dance.

A clumsy deer with feet so wide,
Tramples leaves, but beams with pride.
Crickets cheer, they form a line,
Shaking tails to the soft moonshine.

Chasing shadows, a playful chase,
Laughter echoes, sets the pace.
Each cackle tells of silly schemes,
As romance blooms in leafy dreams.

Oh, what joy the dusk unveils,
Bringing laughter in warm gales.
In this twilight, fun takes flight,
As nature dances through the night!

Beneath the Boughs' Caress

Beneath the boughs, a squirrel prances,
With acorns flying, creating glances.
A wily fox hides in plain sight,
Wearing a mustache, quite the delight.

The rabbits giggle, they share a joke,
A dance-off starts between a frog and a bloke.
The wind whispers secrets, oh what a tease,
While the trees applaud with shivering leaves.

Covert Whispers of the Wild

In the underbrush, a frog croaks loud,
A witty critter, drawing a crowd.
The raccoon sneezes, an unexpected show,
Leaves go flying in a laughter-flow.

A turtle tried running, what a sight,
In slow-motion chaos, it took flight.
The owl snickers, perched high on a limb,
"Who's the fastest? I can't see him!"

The Furtive Dance of Insects

The ants are plotting, oh what a scheme,
In a dance of bustle, they follow a beam.
A ladybug twirls, charming all near,
With a tiny top hat, she spreads cheer.

The beetles bring snacks for a late-night spree,
With disco lights flashing— it's quite the glee.
Crickets beat drums with a rhythmic track,
As friends gather round for this wild knack.

Veiled Figures Amidst the Shrubbery

Behind the bushes, a gnome peeks shy,
With a beard made of moss, he waves goodbye.
A hedgehog rolls over, trying to hide,
With squeaks of laughter, he takes it in stride.

The bees buzz along, choreographing fate,
They bumble and stumble, oh, such a state!
In this woodland theater, all come to see,
The comedy of nature, oh what glee!

Embers of Dusk at the Edge

As the sun dips low, a dance begins,
With squirrels in top hats and feathered fins.
They waltz through the grass, all prim and spry,
While cricket confetti flutters from the sky.

A hedgehog juggles acorns with flair,
And a fox in a bowtie gives a cheeky stare.
The fireflies flicker, their lights like stars,
As laughter spills over like nectar from jars.

Birds wear glasses, perched high on a line,
Sipping sweet nectar like fine vintage wine.
While rabbits debate who's the best at hop,
The dusk holds its breath, not ready to stop.

In the last light's glow, a strange sight appears,
A turtle in sandals, sipping on beers.
With giggles and song, the night takes its course,
In this whimsical world, we find comic force.

The Gnarled Secrets of the Thicket

In the twisted limbs where the secrets reside,
A gnome on a tricycle takes a wild ride.
He honks with glee, a most curious sound,
While owls giggle softly, looking all around.

A badger in spectacles reads silly rhymes,
While hidden away are old marmalade crimes.
The bushes all chuckle, rustling with laughs,
While a timid deer tries on oversized hats.

The trees gossip low, as the breeze carries tales,
Of rabbits in capes who finish their jails.
With stories absurd that stretch far and wide,
The thicket keeps secrets that can't be denied.

At the end of the path where the fireflies race,
You might stumble upon a pie-eating face.
A raccoon with charm, now covered in goo,
In this whimsical world, nothing feels true.

The Enshrouded Echo of Night

In the bushes, voices hum,
A cat complains, a squirrel's drum.
Whispers giggle, leaves take flight,
Who's there lurking in the night?

The moon peeks through with a wink,
A raccoon plots, or so I think.
Nonsense echoes, rustles say,
'Come join us! It's a game we play!'

A shadow darts; was it a bird?
Or the mischievous feline stirred?
With laughter laced in every sound,
Nature's mischief knows no bound!

So raise a glass to eerie sight,
Cheers to the whims of the twilight.
As giggles echo, life's delight,
In the dark where joy takes flight.

Nature's Pantheon of Secrets

Underneath the tangled vines,
A council of critters in fine designs.
A fox in a tie, a badger in shades,
Debating the best of their leafy charades!

A wise old owl with a comical stare,
'Why's the goose honking? Is it a dare?'
Laughter erupts as the weasel joins,
With tales of the garden's hidden coins.

Squirrels debate the acorn's worth,
While mockingbirds sing of their mirth.
The shadows giggle, the moonlight beams,
In nature's playhouse, we follow our dreams.

So if you wander where whispers glide,
Join in the fun, take a side!
In this leafy haven of cheer so bright,
Secrets unfold in the flickering light.

The Lineage of Silent Guardians

Among the branches, watchful eyes,
Owls joke with bats in their cozy ties.
The hedgehog guards a treasure trove,
While the gentle deer tap-dance and rove.

A rabbit claims to be the king,
In a crown of leaves, he's quite the thing.
The stoic trees uplift their boughs,
Nodding to the silliness of their vows.

Laughter bounces from leaf to leaf,
As crickets join in without any grief.
What's this laughter, all so absurd?
Chirpy symphonies, never unheard!

So next you stroll through woods so grand,
Remember the laughter, the silly band.
Guardians of whimsy watch with delight,
In the quiet, they party all night.

Riddles Entangled in the Leaves

A leaf fell down and whispered low,
'What do you get from a tree's big show?'
A twinkle tugs at the breeze,
With riddle rhymes that tease the leaves.

A squirrel laughs, 'I know the trick!
A nut for a joke, and it better be quick!'
Confessions swirl, both wildly spun,
In this arboreal riddle run.

What's green and moves but has no feet?
A bush that dances, isn't that neat?
The raccoons chuckle, 'Let's switch the game!
What's furry, sneaky, and hard to name?'

So gather 'round, let the fun ensue,
In tangled leaves, ideas brew.
With laughter echoing through the trees,
Riddles riff just like the breeze.

Arcane Imprints in the Thicket

In the bushes, something peeks,
A squirrel wearing clownish cheeks.
It juggles acorns, oh what a sight,
While wearing a hat that's pink and bright.

Beneath a branch, a rabbit hops,
With tiny shoes and funny props.
He dances to a tune so rare,
And ties his ears up in the air.

A fox with glasses tries to read,
A map of dreams that's filled with greed.
He loses track, then finds a snack,
And in the end, he can't look back.

As twilight falls, the giggles bloom,
From critters planning mischief's doom.
In secret trails of chortles bright,
The thicket buzzes with pure delight.

Flickers of Nightfall among the Leaves

The leaves whisper of tricks untold,
As fireflies dance, both brave and bold.
A raccoon dons a straggly wig,
And balances on a stumpy jig.

A party planned with nuts and cheese,
Each critter comes in fancy sleeves.
The owl spins tales of zany dreams,
Amidst the laughter, nothing seems.

Bathtub frogs croak in perfect time,
While crickets serenade, oh so sublime.
Each rustling leaf plays a little tune,
Under the light of a froggy moon.

The wacky crew takes center stage,
As backflipping bunnies lose their rage.
The twilight's giggles weave and flow,
In this leaf-laden, joyful show.

The Unseen Trail of Twilight

In the dusk, a mystery grows,
As beacons flicker, who really knows?
A hedgehog shrugs, and starts to hum,
While ants all laugh at a clumsy bum.

The chipmunks plot their wild escape,
Dressed in capes of paper, great shape!
They zip through grass like speeding trains,
In search of snacks and shiny gains.

With beetles rolling mini barrels,
They march with flair, forgetting perils.
The nighttime choir, full of glee,
Turns every moment into a spree.

As laughter echoes and echoes blend,
These antics may never truly end.
For in the dark, the fun's alive,
With all these critters, who'll survive?

Whims of the Hidden Glade

In a glade where secrets dance,
A raccoon finds a stolen chance.
It wears a tutu, twirls with grace,
And sprinkles smiles all over the place.

The hedgehog spins in stolen shoes,
While squirrels chant their funny blues.
Each critter brings a quirky hat,
As they plot tricks with a plump old cat.

Foliage giggles, as shadows sway,
There's mischief brewing in the fray.
The giggly breeze invites a chase,
Amongst the branches, laughter's pace.

In the twilight, joy does prevail,
The garden hums a happy tale.
With silliness tucked in every leaf,
These woodland pals will find no grief.

The Enchantment of Dim Hues

In the underbrush, things gleam,
A sneaky squirrel plotting a scheme.
He juggles acorns, oh what a sight,
Under the cover of fading light.

A rabbit wearing a tiny hat,
Promotes a dance with a sprightly spat.
His friends all giggle, twirl and hop,
As shadows giggle, they cannot stop.

A hedgehog plays a tune on leaves,
While the owl pretends he believes.
And then a fox, so sly, so spry,
Joins in with a twinkling eye.

At dusk, the breeze carries a tune,
As creatures laugh beneath the moon.
In this realm of quirky literary hue,
It's not quite scary—just a bit askew.

Flickering Figures in the Green Abyss

Beneath the branches, things lurk tight,
A dancing snail with a flair for fright.
He slips and slides, red nose aglow,
Just trying to steal the show, you know?

A chipmunk in a cape, feeling grand,
Declares he's the hero of this land.
With a cape made of leaves, he takes a stance,
Unaware he's ruining a squirrel's chance.

A raccoon moonwalks, all suave, no doubt,
He thinks he's the king as he struts about.
But his reflection shows a goofy grin,
One paw in a puddle, letting the fun begin.

As twilight falls, they all convene,
In this comedy of nature, it's quite the scene.
No danger here, just giggles and bliss,
In this woodland dance, who could resist?

Nature's Subtle Intimidation

In the thicket, a bear's not so mean,
He wears a tutu, and he's quite the queen.
As he wobbles and spins with a gentle sway,
The bushes erupt in raucous play.

A boisterous frog jumps, ribbiting loud,
Leaping over branches, feeling so proud.
Yet, he slips on a leaf, oh what a sight,
Flops into the pond, a comedic flight.

A ferret in glasses sips on chamomile,
Claiming it's tea—oh what a style!
With a mustache made from twine and glue,
His friends all giggle at his haute debut.

The sun sets low, and laughter ensues,
While the critters debate their favorite shoes.
In this woods where the oddity reigns,
Nature's absurdity is where joy gains.

The Silent Watch of the Woods

A party of frogs, all dressed in green,
Plotting behind the bushes, like a scene.
They sip sweet nectar from tiny cups,
Mischief is brewing, just look at those pups.

A raccoon stands guard, nose in the air,
With a wink and a grin, he shows his flair.
'Who's brave enough to steal my snack?'
His friends chuckle softly, no sense of lack.

Beneath the ferns, a turtle tries to dance,
His slow-motion moves make all critters prance.
But as he twirls, he stumbles with style,
Leaving laughs echoing for quite a while.

When darkness falls, their laughter fills,
The winding paths, the ancient hills.
No spooky vibes, just pure delight,
In this secret glade of whimsical flight.

Where the Wild Things Lurk.

Just past the gate, they hide and play,
Mischievous critters, on a sunny day.
Socks on their ears and hats a bit askew,
They dance in their gardens, a wild view!

Bouncing like rabbits, they're full of glee,
Tripping on branches, oh what a spree!
Chasing the butterflies, but they run fast,
Where the light fades, their shenanigans last.

They plot little pranks behind trees so wide,
With giggles and hiccups they cannot hide.
One steals a shoe, the other a snack,
A whacky, wild journey, there's never a lack!

As dusk gently falls, they huddle tight,
Trading their tales in the fading light.
With snickers and snorts, they tell of the fun,
In their leafy domain, the wild things run!

Whispers Beneath the Foliage

In the bushes, secrets spin and twirl,
Giggling leaves and a tiny squirrel.
Murmurs of mischief float on the breeze,
As plants share of antics, oh pretty please!

The roses gossip, while daisies just nod,
A tale of a worm who danced with a frog.
Chuckle and chatter, the trees sway along,
Under the cover, they sing a song!

A cat takes a nap on a soft, green bed,
Little do they know—it's all in their head.
For rustles and jeers from beneath the fronds,
Craft a merry tale of cryptic bonds.

As night draws near, they weave out of sight,
With chuckles and wiggles, oh what a sight!
For once the moon peeks, the stories recede,
But the whispers return, as the night's mischief breeds.

Lurking Phantoms of the Garden

In the flower pots, they peek and swirl,
Malicious marigolds give a twirl.
Wily old herbs with an impish grin,
Plotting their pranks, where should we begin?

A toad in a hat hops high up a sprout,
Proclaiming himself the king of the route.
Next to him giggles a sweet little snail,
With plans to release a mysterious veil.

Frogs sing their jingles, loud as a bell,
While shadows keep watch—oh, what a spell!
But wait—what's that? A bee with a crown!
He's zipping and zooming, spinning around!

When the sun fades low, they gather to scheme,
In the garden where laughter dances like steam.
As the fireflies twinkle, their pranks take flight,
In their hidden kingdom, all feels just right!

Secrets of the Leafy Veil

Behind the ferns, mischief quietly waits,
Squirrels in bowties, debating their fate.
With acorns for snacks and twigs for their art,
They're planning a party with flair and heart!

The hedges are bustling, a crafty parade,
With giggles and whispers, the plans are laid.
A raccoon in glasses reads out the rules,
While cacti wear tutus—those prickly fools!

As night gently falls, they orchestrate fun,
With teamwork, they gather; the party's begun.
From twinkling lights to a dance on the grass,
Each critter spins wildly, oh, what a class!

A toast to the night, with dewdrops to sip,
In the midst of their laughter, one takes a trip.
And as they all tumble, amidst giggles and wails,
The secrets of trees dance beneath leafy trails!

Enigmas of the Overgrown Path

Beneath the leaves, the whispers twine,
Are those just branches, or someone's spine?
A squirrel chuckles, or is it a ghost?
Who knew the weeds could host such a roast?

Around the bend, a rustle, a squeak,
The hedges giggle; they play hide and seek.
Is that a shadow, or just my friend?
I swear, these bushes have secrets to lend!

Look at that fern, a sneaky little chap,
Wearing a mask, in a leafy mishap.
Are they all plotting a grand prank tonight?
Quick! Grab the camera before they take flight!

But wait, what's that? A footpath all snug,
Where raccoons gather for a wild hug.
With silly antics that spin in the air,
These grassy conspirators dance without care!

Glistening Dark Beneath the Branches

In the thick of night, the giggles abound,
What's that? A treasure, or just the ground?
A beetle twirls, wearing a shiny coat,
Is that its dance, or a crazy boat?

The night sky sparkles like questions unknown,
With laughter creeping through bushes overgrown.
Are those just fireflies, or tiny star thieves?
They flicker and flitter like mischief achieves!

A rustle breaks forth, a comical sight,
A hedgehog in glasses, studying the night.
He claims he's a scholar of the garden's own,
Writing a thesis on a potato's tone!

So tiptoe a bit through this playful maze,
Where nature giggles and winks in a daze.
With each step taken, the fun's just begun,
In the glistening dark, let's all be undone!

Veils of Green and Gray

In layers of green, the fun tends to hide,
A raccoon decides to take us for a ride.
With bags packed full of acorns and cheese,
He winks and invites us to come if we please.

A gust of wind, and the bushes start to sway,
Is that a dance team or some kind of play?
With leaves all around, it's a comical scene,
The overgrown path turns a tad too obscene!

A snail on a mission, slow, but so wise,
He says, "Don't rush, keep your eyes on the prize."
With laughter erupting from every small nook,
Could nature be writing its own little book?

Through veils of green and a touch of gray,
The laughter of creatures won't fade away.
So step into this world where the humor runs free,
In the playful embrace of the plants and the trees!

Unseen Watchers in the Underbrush

A twitch of a tail, what could it be now?
Is there a party in the garden? Oh wow!
The crickets are singing, adding to the cheer,
With every chirp, they dance, oh dear!

Bamboo is nodding, as if to the beat,
Inviting all critters for a nighttime treat.
A raccoon magician pulls snacks from thin air,
His furry little hands causing giggles to flare!

What's hidden beneath the cloak of the leaves?
An audience chuckling, who knows what it weaves?
With laughter erupting and jumps that draw gasps,
These unseen watchers are friendship's true rasps!

So gather around in this vibrant green space,
Where giggles and whispers invite us to race.
In the underbrush, let's share hearty laughs,
With unseen companions in their comical halves!

Beneath the Murmuring Leaves

In the garden, giggles sprout,
As squirrels dance about.
They hide nuts in secret spots,
Plotting snacks, oh what a lot!

A rabbit wears a tiny hat,
Chasing shadows, oh imagine that!
With every hop, a little prance,
In the thicket, they all dance!

The breeze whispers a silly tune,
Underneath the dappled moon.
Funny frogs with trumpet sounds,
Joke and jive while spring abounds!

Giggling leaves above our heads,
Tickle grass and tease the beds.
The garden's charm, a laugh we share,
In this leafy world, free from care!

The Hidden Realm of Starlit Leaves

At dusk, the fireflies play tag,
While toads leap with a little wag.
In the dark, they play their games,
Whispering loud, with silly names!

Oh, the owls wear glasses, you see,
Reading tales of mystery!
Chirping crickets keep the beat,
As the night unfolds its sweet treat.

A raccoon juggles under the moon,
With all the finesse of a cartoon.
While hedgehogs roll in fits of glee,
Sneaky, yet as cute as can be!

The stars giggle at the scene,
Watching antics with a sheen.
Each leaf holds a funny spark,
Lighting up the world, oh what a lark!

Gaze of the Gloomy Grove

In the grove, the owls hoot,
Wearing beards, they look quite cute.
The trees lean in with gnarled faces,
Peeking through the little spaces.

A caterpillar in a chair,
Counting bugs with flair and care.
As mushrooms giggle, high and proud,
Underneath the foggy shroud.

Each cranny holds a playful jest,
With will-o'-the-wisps on a quest.
They lead the way with flickering light,
Chasing giggles into the night.

What mischief lingers in the air?
Whispers of fun everywhere.
With every turn, laughter rings,
In the tale that twilight brings!

Secrets Woven in the Green

In the thicket, tales arise,
Of mischievous little spies.
A hedgehog claims the best of spots,
Fighting off a band of pots.

The bushes chuckle, leaves in pairs,
Woven stories, mixed with cares.
A raccoon steals from his own stash,
Causing quite a silly clash!

With tangled vines under the stars,
Frogs bounce high, ignoring cars.
The branches sway, a leafy choir,
Singing songs of pure desire.

And as the sun dips low and down,
The grove transforms, leaves in a gown.
With laughter echoing, light as air,
It's a realm of joy, beyond compare!

Vandals of the Verdant Silence

In the thicket, giggles grow,
Squirrels plotting, oh what a show!
They steal the acorns, hide them away,
While rabbits dance, hip-hop ballet.

A raccoon dons a mischievous grin,
With pizza crusts he's found within.
Chirping crickets join the feast,
As shadows bounce, to say the least.

A turtle thinks he's quite the star,
With leafy hats from near and far.
The bushes rustle, laughter bright,
As critters play through day and night.

Among the leaves, a prankster's scheme,
A flower's hat—a wild dream!
Nature's jesters, bold and spry,
In this green world, they soar and fly.

Beneath the Canopy's Enigma

Under the leaves, a secret plot,
A gopher swipes a donut—hot!
While owls squint with eyes so wide,
Watching chaos they can't abide.

A fox in sneakers starts to zoom,
Dancing wildly—what a room!
While beetles dress in suits so grand,
Strutting their stuff with a band.

Beneath the boughs, a wild charade,
With laughter spilled like lemonade.
The winds whisper jokes, so sly,
As nature chuckles, oh my, oh my!

A spider spins some tangled threads,
Wrapping up dreams in silken beds.
With each twist, it seems to cheer,
As creatures laugh from ear to ear.

The Cryptic Aura of the Glade

In the glade where whispers hum,
A deer does tap dance—look at him!
With branches clapping, all in sync,
They laugh and chuckle, never blink.

A porcupine, with quills on show,
Starts a band—oh what a blow!
The fireflies provide the light,
As everyone jams into the night.

Suddenly a raccoon trips a hare,
They tumble 'round without a care.
In this whimsical, leafy space,
The creatures wear a goofy face.

An owl brings jokes, a shining star,
With puns so bad, they raise a bar.
In every nook, the laughter flows,
A goofy crew, with no repose.

Penumbral Characters in Nature's Play

We find the jesters in the gloom,
With hedgehogs dancing to a tune.
While shadows stretch and twist about,
A crabapple's face wears a pout.

A mole shows off his freestyle moves,
As the daisies tap with grooves.
While butterflies whisper gossip so grand,
Caterpillars start a marching band.

The woodpecker drums on the hollow tree,
Counting beats, one, two, three!
As all the creatures take their place,
In this playful, green embrace.

With laughter bursting from each bough,
The forest holds its funny vow.
Beneath the stars, their fun won't wane,
In nature's dance, they'll entertain!

Colloquy of Lights and Shadows

In the park, the glow shines bright,
A squirrel dances out of sight.
With a leap and a twist, it seems,
To join in on my silly dreams.

Beneath the trees, a giggle hides,
Where missed step is where joy resides.
The pasty light with playful bends,
Whispers secrets like old friends.

From the bushes, a rustle—no,
Just a cat with an ego to show.
It struts with grace, a thespian's flair,
Steals the show without a care.

As moonlit pranks begin to play,
Just watch the shadows on their way.
A comedy of forms and sights,
In the mischievous dance of nights.

The Obscured Path of the Unknown

The trail ahead is dimly lit,
With giggles and whispers that don't quite fit.
Nature's jesters hide and seek,
In the undergrowth, a playful peek.

A rustling leaf, a sudden squeal,
What lurks behind? Is it surreal?
A bunny or a troll in disguise,
Trading folly for eager eyes.

I tiptoe or I bounce, unsure,
Of the antics that nature has in store.
The bushes giggle, the brambles tease,
While laughter dances upon the breeze.

I step again; the world seems strange,
Each turn reveals a playful change.
With every giggle, the night unfolds,
Revealing humor that never grows old.

Enigmatic Rustle in the Twilight

Through the twilight, whispers call,
A tumble down, a squirrel's fall.
Mischief reigns where the laughter's loud,
As the forest dons a playful shroud.

A branch creaks—who could it be?
A shadowy figure or just a tree?
The bushes sway in a gentle dance,
Playing tricks in a lively trance.

Chirps and chuckles fill the air,
As critters chuck confetti with flair.
A hedgehog dons a cap and eyes,
Throwing glances with sleepy sighs.

In the laughter, time stands still,
The world transforms at its own will.
Embracing quirks in the fading light,
Twilight plays its favorite bite.

Lurkers of the Fragrant Brush

Amidst the blooms, the mischief brews,
A hidden gaggle of wily snooze.
With petals prancing, they unfold,
The secrets of folly yearning to be told.

A mouse yells, 'Stop! Who goes there?'
In the brush, a curious stare.
A chorus of giggles fills the night,
As flora plots in delight.

In this corner, the bumblebees buzz,
Flirting with blooms, creating a fuzz.
While ladybugs grin, feeling grand,
Narrating tales in this whimsical land.

Each moment holds a jest or trick,
In this fragrant world, where shadows pick.
A frolic in the night, come what may,
In the garden where mischief loves to play.

Outlines of Dusk in the Shrubland

In the hush of twilight's grace,
A squirrel does a silly chase,
With shadows playing peek-a-boo,
The bushes giggle just for you.

A bird sneezes, then takes flight,
It startles a hedgehog, what a sight!
The leaves chuckle, rustling low,
As crickets start their evening show.

A cat leaps with a pounce and wiggle,
The bushes shake, they seem to giggle,
A mischief made by twilight's hand,
Where laughter dances through the land.

As night wraps close and whispers cheer,
The animals toast with frothy beer,
Amidst the green, we find our thrill,
In nocturnal fun, we sip our fill.

The Watchful Eyes of the Underbrush

Creepy-crawly eyes awake,
Peeking through the bushes, what a rake!
A rabbit winks from his leafy seat,
While a raccoon taps his furry feet.

The flowers gossip, petals quirk,
As ants march in, their little work,
Mice scurry, their tails like whips,
In the underbrush, they share their quips.

A thistle plays a mischievous role,
While toads croak tunes on a leafy stroll,
Every rustle tells a joke anew,
Between the branches, laughter flew.

Oh, these characters of lush delight,
All gather under the moon's soft light,
With eyes a-twinkle, bright and wide,
In the underbrush, they take their pride.

The Cryptic Dance of Darkness

The night unfolds with a sway and spin,
As mice and shadows gather in,
They twist and twirl in cloak of gloom,
In the dark, they find a room.

A fox wearing spectacles, quite the sight,
Conducts the dance with all his might,
The owls hoot with rhythmic thrill,
While fireflies buzz their lanterns still.

A leaf caught in a waltz so grand,
Flutters and flutters, slips from hand,
The moonlight laughs, it shines so bright,
While crickets chirp, a tune of night.

With every whisper, every cackle,
The ghost of darkness plays a tackle,
In the twilight's grip, we find our way,
In giggles and glee, we dance and sway.

Ghosts of Flora and Fauna

Beneath the fronds where fancies lurk,
Silly spirits start their work,
Bumblebees buzz with a spectral grin,
As flowers sip on moonlight's gin.

A moth wearing shades flutters about,
Dancing with shadows that twist and shout,
The daisies hum a tune so sweet,
While the breeze taps to the steady beat.

The thorns relate their ghostly tales,
Of mischief played by little snails,
Lurking roots wrapped in a prank,
A leafy bandit, an emerald prank.

In the brush, the laughter swells,
With every rustle, cheeky spells,
The hints of whimsy fill the night,
As nature's jesters take to flight.

Slumbering Echoes of the Earth

Beneath the leafy covers fast,
The creatures play and hide at last.
A fox with boots, a squirrel in socks,
Dance around the laughing rocks.

The toads are croaking silly tunes,
While daisies sway like silly loons.
A beetle joins with tap-tap feet,
Their joy a sound, a merry beat.

While ants march in a conga line,
The sun dips low, they sip on wine.
A picnic feast of crumbs and crumbs,
Where every bite leads to more fun.

As night descends, the giggles grow,
An owl winks with a wise, "You know?"
In dreams of laughter, they will twirl,
In slumber's arms, the world's a whirl.

Secrets Breaching Through the Veil

Whispers in the glowing dark,
A raccoon paints with a spark.
He claims the moon as his own prize,
While crickets giggle with bright eyes.

A hedgehog dons a tiny hat,
Pretending he's a clever cat.
The bushes rustle, secrets keep,
As midnight mischief wakes from sleep.

A squirrel with tales of acorn stash,
Boasts of adventures with a dash.
The others laugh, they chime in too,
With wild stories of who they knew.

Under a blanket made of leaves,
A council forms, each one believes.
That there's more fun to find at night,
As secrets dance in soft moonlight.

The Green Tapestry of Twilight

In twilight's glow, the colors blend,
A gnome with shoes begins to bend.
He plants a joke in the ground so neat,
And sprinkles laughter with tiny feet.

A rabbit hops with carrot pride,
Wears shades as if he's on a ride.
The world becomes a canvas bright,
As colors pulse in fading light.

A patchwork quilt of giggle schemes,
A firefly brightens everyone's dreams.
As fireflies twirl and frogs all cheer,
The laughter echoes, loud and clear.

Amidst the greens, the fun is spread,
With each non-serious tale they've read.
In the tapestry of dusk's embrace,
They weave their joys, a playful space.

Lament of the Hidden Grove

In the grove where whispers play,
The trees reveal their funny sway.
A squirrel spins tales of furry glee,
In every rustle, a new decree.

The bushes giggle, leaves a-flutter,
While snails are having quite the clutter.
Each bloom a character in a jest,
They all agree this is the best.

A bear in slippers takes a stroll,
He trips on roots and starts to roll.
The larks above can barely sing,
As laughter erupts from everything.

So in the grove where secrets spill,
Each creature laughs and shares a thrill.
For even in a hidden space,
The joy of jest holds its warm place.

Whispers Beneath the Leaves

Beneath the boughs, a rustle heard,
A squirrel plots, not one word stirred.
Is it a joke, or maybe a prank?
The raccoons giggle, they're in on the prank.

But wait! What's that? A twig does snap,
A hedgehog stumbles, takes a quick nap.
The laughter stirs, the breeze takes flight,
In this leafy town, all's twilight delight.

With acorns flying, what a mess,
The bunnies hop and feel quite blessed.
A chase ensues, a slapstick play,
In the underbrush, they dance all day.

So whisper low, don't disrupt the cheer,
For in this greenery, fun draws near.
The creatures laugh, a silly brigade,
In nature's comedy, they're unafraid.

Echoes Among the Thicket

In the thicket's heart, a giggle breaks,
Two foxes plot what the crow forsakes.
With tricks so sly, a crafty display,
They make a game of the light of day.

The owls hoot twice, they crack a smile,
As rabbits bounce, like clowns for a while.
With every leap, a giggle follows,
Through branches thick, and grassy hollows.

Bees play tag with flowers in bloom,
While butterflies dance, dispelling the gloom.
A caterpillar rolls, brings laughs all around,
In this leafy corner, joy knows no bound.

So listen close, for the sounds of cheer,
Echo through the thicket, loud and clear.
In nature's play, each creature is bold,
Amusement thrives in stories untold.

The Veil of Twilight Flora

As night descends, the giggles ignite,
A chameleon twirls, a colorful sight.
The fireflies blink, like stars in a mess,
To dance among flowers in frilly dress.

A turtle lumbers, with style so grand,
Claims he can out-hop the best in the land.
The frogs croak loudly, all full of zest,
At the finish line, they put him to rest.

With blooms so bright, and laughter in air,
The hedgehogs tangle, in a messy affair.
But oh, what fun, under the moon's glow,
In this world of laughter, it's all just for show.

So join the revels, embrace the spree,
For under the flora, we're wild and free.
With mirth and delight, the night unfolds,
In twilight gardens, where joy never cold.

Secrets Among the Greenery

In the greenery thick, with secrets to share,
A rabbit tells tales, with sass and flair.
A badger bursts out, can't hold a grin,
"There's treasure there," and the chaos begins.

Through bushes they tumble, in search of the loot,
While a wise old owl says, "What's the root?"
The critters all laugh, forgetting the quest,
For jokes on the trail are truly the best.

The grass now a stage, for a play so fine,
Where beetles perform with a touch of divine.
The giggles resound as each act takes place,
In nature's own theater, there's ample space.

So cherish the chuckles, let whimsy take flight,
For secrets abound in the soft moonlight.
With joy as our guide in each leafy scene,
Among the green, we create the unseen.

Silenced Voices within the Thicket

Little critters start to chatter,
Squirrels plotting, oh what a matter!
Bushy tails flick, a secret affair,
Who stole the acorns? Beware, beware!

A hedgehog whispers, "Not me, you see!"
While rabbits giggle, as bold as can be.
The owl just hoots, a wise old face,
In the leafy world, it's a funny place!

Here's a dance-off in the tangled green,
With dance moves only a frog could deem.
Toads join in with a ribbit and hop,
Who knew the thicket could be such a bop!

But hush now friends, the cat is near,
A stealthy hunter with a flick of ear.
In this green maze, where laughter unwinds,
Nature's antics bring joy to our minds.

Subtle Currents of Dusk's Caress

As twilight spreads a gentle cheer,
Mice hold party snacks, drawing near.
A dance of fireflies lights up the gloam,
While frogs croak tunes that feel like home.

Chirping crickets share their best jokes,
While the fox laughs, rolling with the folks.
In the dusky light, the fun rolls on,
Under the trees, until the dawn.

The tiny bugs with their glowing butts,
Have formed a conga line to the rustling nuts.
The raccoon joins with a mask of glee,
Doing the twist like a wild spree!

But wait—a rustle, what could it be?
A sneaky creature with snackery glee!
They scatter and giggle, what a fun chase,
Dusk's playful dance is a wild embrace.

The Hidden Compass of Nature

In the glen where the wild things play,
A compass lost, in disarray.
The squirrel spins, directing the lot,
"Let's find the treasure!"—a nutty plot.

Fungi point with an eerie glow,
While beetles pinch at the seeds they stow.
Follow the trail of bright, sneaky ants,
Leading us all to mysterious plants!

The mossy map shows paths so funny,
"Left at the brook, then to the honey!"
Through tangled vines and dancing leaves,
Adventures arise like wild, merry thieves.

An uncharted world full of surprise,
Nature's own pirates all find their prize.
With laughter and cheer, they gather near,
This hidden quest, a haven sincere.

Whispers of the Woodland Spirit

In the heart of the woods, a giggle flows,
A spirit chuckles where the wild rose grows.
Tap-dancing fairies under the moon,
Turning the night into a catchy tune.

The badger dances, with glasses askew,
While acorns roll, it's a most comical view!
"Oops, a spill!" the raccoon does say,
As seeds take flight in a playful ballet.

With branches swaying to a woodland beat,
And critters jiving on hilarious feet,
Mushroom hats bobbing as they jauntily sway,
Nature's frolics make a joyous display!

So listen closely, it's true, it's clear,
The woodland spirit holds laughter dear.
In every rustle, a chuckle you'll find,
In the grand, leafy world, we're all intertwined.

Nature's Half-Light Secrets

In the garden, once so bright,
Creatures play by fading light.
A squirrel dons a cap, not neat,
And dances on its tiny feet.

Bunnies hop with such delight,
Thinking it's still broad daylight.
The birds sing out a goofy tune,
While bats prepare to join the moon.

A hedgehog sneezes, causing cheer,
As crickets strum a song sincere.
The flowers giggle, petals sway,
Who knew dusk could be so play?

Let us wander, laugh and spin,
In the twilight where fun begins.
Nature's secrets, oh so bright,
Make us chuckle in the night.

The Concealed Embrace of Branches

Underneath the leafy dome,
Squirrels plot where best to roam.
A branch drops down, but look, oh dear,
Turns out it's just a bucket here!

With slumbering owls and grumpy bears,
All very hush, without some cares.
A raccoon steals a lunch for fun,
With taco dreams, it claims it won.

The wise old tree has stories told,
Of mischief wrought and antics bold.
But when you peek, alas, you find,
A cactus sneezed—now that's unkind!

So laugh, my friend, in this leafy space,
For whimsy thrives in nature's grace.
With twists and turns, let joy expand,
Embrace the chuckles, hand in hand.

Intricate Patterns in the Dusk

In the gloom, odd shapes appear,
Dancing shadows, causing cheer.
A toad hops in a dainty waltz,
While crickets laugh at their own faults.

Butterflies, wearing tiny hats,
Join the fun with sassy chats.
The fireflies flicker, twinkling bright,
Making it feel like a fancy night.

But hold on tight, for what's that sound?
A frog that croaks—a mischief found!
He trips on leaves, a comic show,
As laughter echoes—hey, let's go!

In this moment of silly dreams,
Together we shall burst at seams.
With nature's charm, we giggle and sway,
Creating joy at end of day.

The Cloak of Secretive Ferns

Crouched beneath the fronds and curls,
We find our way in leafy swirls.
A snail with swagger, slow parade,
Claims it's the king of this green shade!

The bushes rustle with secret glee,
As ants hold court in revelry.
The ferns whisper jokes, oh so sly,
While spiders strum their webs nearby.

A lizard's doing yoga, you see,
Stretching limbs, feeling so free.
And if you listen—oh, what a sound!
The frog's off-key, but we still clown.

So let us dance with leaves above,
In a world that feels so full of love.
With laughter weaving through the greens,
Embrace the joy of woodland scenes.

Shadows Unspooled in the Garden

In the tall grass, something twitched,
A squirrel in a hat, oh what a pitch!
He danced on a stone, felt quite refined,
While daisies chuckled, their petals entwined.

A rabbit approached, sporting a tie,
Challenging him, with a wink in his eye.
Together they jived, both quirky and spry,
As the flowers rolled over, not shy to comply.

The bees buzzed along, with a rhythm so sweet,
As they joined the dance, oh what a treat!
In the garden's embrace, the laughter took flight,
Creating a scene, oh what pure delight!

When dusk approached, they took a bow,
With all of nature cheering, here and now.
Who knew the garden could be so grand?
With jesters and laughter, hand in hand!

Murky Whispers in the Foliage

Beneath leafy hats, secrets were spread,
A lizard in glasses, quite well-read.
He pondered the mysteries of dandelion tea,
While pondering why squirrels had fancy esprit.

The bushes giggled, sharing tall tales,
Of gnomes on the run, wielding their pails.
A hedgehog, still snoozing, missed all the fun,
Dreaming of pizza, a slice to be won.

A crow flew by, who just had to squawk,
About how the critters had all learned to talk.
"Yet here I am," he cawed with a flair,
"Just trying to steal some romantics out there!"

With a rustle and shuffle, they plotted some pranks,
As shadows danced wildly and giggled in ranks.
In the murky green, where laughter does thrive,
The characters thrived in their quest to survive!

Stilled Breath of the Hidden Realm

In the nook of the bushes, some critters conspired,
To hold a grand meeting, all quite inspired.
A mole brought the chips, while a fox led the way,
With munchies galore to brighten the day!

A hedgehog claimed he could juggle three nuts,
While the ants cheered him on, giving loud shouts.
They laughed and they giggled till the moon shone bright,

As bats flew overhead, causing quite the fright!

A turtle rolled in, with a top hat so tall,
Claiming to be the magician of all!
He pulled out a flower, a trick so absurd,
And the crowd erupted, their giggles unheard.

With the night wearing on, they crafted their schemes,
Sharing silly stories, and outlandish dreams.
In the hidden realm, with spirits so light,
The night ended happily, all felt just right!

Unraveled Paths Amidst the Growth

In the labyrinth deep, where the vines intertwine,
An owl gave directions, or was it just wine?
The bunnies threw parties, balloons in the air,
While toadstools played music, a real wild affair.

The paths twisted wildly, they giggled and spun,
Searching for treasures, oh what glorious fun!
A raccoon in overalls measured the space,
As he accidentally tripped, fell flat on his face.

A ladybug chuckled, giving him cheer,
"Get up, dear friend, you're a sight, let's be clear!"
So they danced through the night, forgoes had been made,

In a whirlwind of laughter, the path just displayed.

When morn brushed the leaves with its soft, gentle kiss,
The critters still giggled, recalling their bliss.
In unraveled pathways, where joy was a must,
The garden lived on, quite vibrant and just!

Silken Shadows on Fern Fronds

A wily fox with a sly little grin,
Sneaks through the ferns, oh where have you been?
With whispers of mischief, and rustles of fun,
He tiptoes in twilight, just on the run.

A rabbit nearby, with fur all a-fluff,
Hears giggles and chuckles, finds it quite tough.
She puffs up her cheeks, and with one little hop,
Crashes through leaves, making all the tops stop!

The owls hear the ruckus, they hoot with delight,
As the dancers prance under the pale moonlight.
The night may be fraught with its eerie surprise,
But laughter and antics can brighten the skies.

So if you should wander, just keep your eyes peeled,
For joyful mischief is truly revealed.
In the flip of a tail or a rustling leaf,
You'll find that the night hides pure comic relief.

Mysterious Forms in the Tangle

In the thicket where whispers meet glee with despair,
Slinking shapes prance, with colors so rare.
A hedgehog in glasses reads poetry loud,
While squirrels debate how to best form a crowd.

A tangle of vines, a commune of gags,
They gossip of starlight and wiggle their rags.
A laugh from the underbrush jolts all dismay,
As chipmunks play tricks, flinging acorns their way.

The bushes they shuffle, a parade on the go,
While critters do cartwheels, putting on quite a show.
Every rustle ignites a chuckle so sweet,
As creatures collide in this whimsical feat.

Beneath leafy curtains, the antics unfold,
In the dance of the night, where all can be bold.
If you peer through the branches, you might just hear,
The sound of life laughing, so vibrant and clear.

The Lurk of Verdant Mystery

Amidst leafy labyrinths, a giggle runs fast,
While a panda in plaid tries to blend in at last.
He twirls and he jigs, all silly and bold,
In hopes of a snack, or some stories retold.

A raccoon takes charge with a mischievous grin,
He spins tales of treasures and where they've been.
Each rustle and chuckle makes everyone squeal,
With laughter and folly, the forest does reel.

A conga line starts, a mix-up of paws,
With partners unchosen, and dances that pause.
They trip on their feet, yet they tumble with cheer,
Making friends through the fumbles, that's how it appears.

As night wraps around, the antics don't fade,
With flashes of fun, and each spectacle made.
Join in on the frolics beyond the green scene,
For laughter is living, wherever you've been.

Hushed Footsteps in the Wilderness

Beneath the tall branches, where silence can dwell,
Dare the footsteps of forest critters to swell.
A turtle in boots takes a very small stride,
While giggling mice dart in a mad little ride.

The trees cast their brows as they witness the jest,
With fables of clumsiness dressed in their best.
Each whispering breeze holds a secret in tow,
Where squirrels drop nuts that just won't even flow.

A hedgehog escapes with a jump and a squeak,
While rabbits in scarves play hide-and-seek.
The shadows grow longer, a silly parade,
As giggles erupt in the green masquerade.

So venture where footsteps may skip or may slide,
Where chuckles and whispers know how to collide.
In the hush of the wild, find the joy that reclaims,
For wilderness thrums with the pulse of their games.

Illusions of the Midnight Grove

In the grove where cool winds dance,
Laughter echoes, a quirky chance.
A raccoon juggling pinecones so bright,
While owls roll their eyes at the sight.

Fireflies flash like errant sparks,
A squirrel debates with the trees and larks.
Their arguments loud, yet nobody cares,
As the moon snickers, revealing their flares.

The fox wears a hat, quite absurd indeed,
Claiming it's fashion, not just by need.
While hedgehogs gossip and share their woes,
Plotting who wins the next great pose.

So come join the fun in this loony place,
Where whimsy reigns and giggles race.
Each corner holds a jest or two,
Here in the grove, where laughter is true.

Mirage of the Enchanted Thicket

In the thicket, a sound like sneezing,
Turns out it's just a bear, a bit too wheezy.
He tries to dance but stumbles around,
Crashing twigs with a comical sound.

The bunnies giggle, their tails like puffs,
As the bear trails off with his wobbly huffs.
"They call that a dance?" one little voice cried,
"More like a wobble!" they cackled, then sighed.

The raccoon with coffee, perched on a log,
Sips his brew and feels like a cog.
"A party tonight, everyone's here!"
Then trips on the root and spills all his cheer.

Now the night holds all sorts of blunders,
As creatures gather, bursting with wonders.
With chuckles and guffaws, it's a merry affair,
In the thicket of mirage, without a care.

Sable Tendrils of Nightfall

In the grasp of the twilight, a dance starts to form,
Where the owls just want to munch on a worm.
A cat struts by in a cloak of sleek black,
With dreams of a dinner, but hunger does lack.

A toad croaks loudly, claims he's a bard,
With tunes so outlandish, they're often quite hard.
Yet frogs join the chorus with legs in a jig,
Creating a jam out of hopping and gig.

The night critters chuckle, a raucous delight,
As stars twinkle back, joining the sight.
"Who's that?" asks the hedgehog, bemused in their glee,
"Just our dancing pal, he's a bit hard to see!"

So gather your friends, let's revel in cheer,
In the sable embrace where laughter is near.
A noodle of fun in the dark of the night,
Where giggles abound, oh what a sight!

Veiled Mysteries of the Gloom

In the gloom where mischief grows wild and free,
A frog whispers secrets to a curious bee.
The laughter erupts, then falls to a hush,
As tiny feet thrum in a magical rush.

A dragonfly claims it can soar like a kite,
While ants roll in grass, what a comical sight!
"Let's build us a castle!" the cricket does say,
But halfway through building, they lose their way.

The moon's got a grin, shining down on the spree,
While fireflies blink like a star-studded sea.
"Dance with us now," calls a spider on high,
"Or miss out on folly that floats through the sky!"

So if you should wander where wonders all bloom,
Join the night creatures, banish your gloom.
For in hidden corners, the humor will gleam,
In veiled mysteries, life wears a dream.

The Twilight's Cloak in the Grove

In the glimmering dusk, what a sight,
A squirrel in a hat, what a delight!
Bouncing from branches, it plays the fool,
Turning the grove into a jolly school.

Leaves dance around, each twist and swirl,
With whispers of mischief, they twirl and twirl.
The moon peeks in, catches a joke,
As raccoons break-dance, in shadows they poke.

A misfit fox joins the dinner feast,
Chasing its own tail like a lively beast.
The laughter of crickets joins in the fun,
As night drapes all under its sparkling run.

What mysteries here, in the night, unfold,
With secrets of nature, both jolly and bold.
But really, who could blame the merry spree?
In the twilight's cloak, all are wild and free!

Mysterious Shapes Behind the Shrubs

What lurks behind, in the bushes tight?
Is it a rabbit, or just a kite?
A garden gnome with a crooked grin,
Plans to steal snacks, who knows what's within?

Bumps and lumps dance in the night,
Raccoon pirates, ready to bite!
They gather around a (not) secret stash,
Sharing tales of candy and an epic clash.

With giggles and hiccups, they hoot and cheer,
Under the watch of the wise old deer.
What a masquerade beneath the stars,
Laughter spills over, echoing far.

In the shadows, fun rules the ground,
As mischief hides where no one is found.
So peek through the leaves, perhaps you'll see,
The giggles of critters, wild and free!

Hushed Breaths in the Verdant Hedges

In the green maze, whispers softly glide,
A hedgehog prances, with great pride!
It twirls past bushes, with fanciful flair,
Thinking, of course, it's winning the dare.

The ferns all chuckle, rustling with glee,
While ants play catch, as lively as can be.
Mice are the judges, giving grand scores,
For each little tumble, they just want more!

Off in the corner, a turtle gets stuck,
In a leafy tangle, oh what bad luck!
But laughter brings all, to help find a way,
In this quirky dance, nature's own play.

Beneath the moon's gaze, giggles abound,
As every crevice, holds fun all around.
So join in the frolic, let your heart sing,
In the evergreen trails, where mirth takes wing!

Eclipsed by Nature's Embrace

Under the twinkling stars, with a wink,
A pebble wobbles at the edge of the brink.
It rolls on its belly, what a funny sight,
Teaching old turtles how to party all night!

The moonlight tickles leaves, oh such a prank,
As shadows throw parties, on the riverbank.
Fish splash around playing leapfrog with ease,
While frogs croak laughter, in a chorus of cheese.

A raccoon in sunglasses surveys the ground,
Sipping on sap, the coolest around!
With beetles breakdancing, and crickets on drums,
Nature's own nightlife is packed full of fun!

In this wild theater, joy takes its place,
As the sun takes a bow, in Nature's embrace.
So dance with the fireflies, sing with delight,
For every small creature has a role in the night!

Murmurs of the Hidden Grove

In the thicket where whispers play,
Squirrels gossip about the day.
A raccoon wears a crown of leaves,
Declaring it's time for pranks and heaves.

Beneath the twigs, a rabbit twirls,
With a carrot made of pearls and curls.
Trees chuckle at the mischief bright,
In the evening's dim, giggles take flight.

The owls wink with a mischievous glance,
As the crickets start their nightly dance.
A fox in a waistcoat tips his hat,
To the kudzu that plays hide and chat.

At dusk, the world begins to tease,
Flowers shiver in the evening breeze.
In this quiet, playful space,
Nature's tricks bring a smiling face.

Enigmas Wrapped in Vines

In a tangle of green where secrets dwell,
A lizard mimics a jolly bell.
Grapes giggle as they dangle low,
Challenging birds in a silly show.

Frantically, the ants march in line,
Debating if crumbs taste better than wine.
Beneath the leaves, a turtle grins wide,
As he hosts the weekly snail slide.

Vines twist around in a playful game,
Mocking their neighbors with silly names.
When sunlight shifts through the leafy haze,
Even the thorns seem to dance and praise.

And just when the night begins to creep,
A bat swoops low while the critters leap.
In this jungle of giggles and glee,
Nature laughs, oh so joyously free.

Dances of the Dusky Green

In the twilight, giggles bounce,
As frogs leap high, while crickets prance.
A hedgehog dons a sparkly coat,
Trying hard to stay afloat.

Twisting branches shake with mirth,
As fireflies twinkle, showing worth.
A family of raccoons in a conga line,
Evaluate the shine of moonlit wine.

The mushrooms whisper secrets untold,
In the game of tag, they're very bold.
Beneath the stars, the night takes charge,
Where mischief and laughter grow large.

Swaying grassfields join the cheer,
As the night creatures hold each dear.
When dawn eventually claims the scene,
Nature smiles, it's been a dream.

Lurkers Beneath the Canopy

In the layers where laughter hides,
Worms tell tales of fun-filled rides.
A beetle struts in shiny shoes,
While ladybugs giggle at the news.

Chattering leaves create a show,
With secrets only the wind can know.
An old tree stump hosts an owl's ball,
As woodland critters heed the call.

At the foot of ferns, ants plot their schemes,
Dancing to the hum of their wild dreams.
A chatty sparrow shouts a rhyme,
Saying it's always a perfect time.

When the moon shines through branches thick,
The hidden creatures play their trick.
In this world of whispers and glee,
Nature's jesters, wild and free.

www.ingramcontent.com/pod-product-compliance
Lightning Source LLC
Chambersburg PA
CBHW071836160426
43209CB00003B/318